REFLE

THINK

REFLECTIONS
THINK ON CHRIST

A month's Meditations

on

Matthew's Gospel

by

Cyril Franks

NCEC

To my wife, who has shared these writings with me.

Cover photo: Robert Bruce
Artwork: Rosi Drew – One And A Half Graphics

Acknowledgements

The editor and publishers acknowledge permission to reproduce the following copyright material:

Bible verses are from the *Good News Bible* (The Bible Societies/Collins Publishers) – New Testament © American Bible Society 1966, 1971, 1976.

Published by:
National Christian Education Council
Robert Denholm House
Nutfield
Redhill RH1 4HW

British Library Cataloguing-in-Publication Data:
Franks, Cyril
Reflections.
1. Bible. N. T. Matthew - Devotional Works
I. Title II. National Christian Education Council
242.5

ISBN 0-7197-0705-6

First published 1991

Typesetting by One And A Half Graphics, Redhill, Surrey
Printed in Great Britain by BPCC-AUP Aberdeen Ltd.

CONTENTS

Matthew 3.1-3

At that time John the Baptist came to the desert of Judaea and started preaching. 'Turn away from your sins,' he said, 'because the Kingdom of heaven is near!' John was the man the prophet Isaiah was talking about when he said,

'Someone is shouting in the desert,
Prepare a road for the Lord;
make a straight path for him to travel!'

Think on Christ

DAY 1

PREPARING THE WAY

Prepare a way for the Lord! Could ever a man have had such an honourable task? Here was a piece of work that, if it had been executed badly, would have resulted in a world damaged, distorted, perhaps even destroyed; but it was done well and the way was opened up for Jesus to serve all creation.

Here He calls me to open a way for Him
  to that bewildered girl, that He may bring peace;
  to that despairing man, that He may give him hope;
  to that bereaved family, that He may bring them comfort;
  to that . . .

It is a heavy burden to think that I am responsible for opening a way for Jesus into anyone's life, but what a privilege, and what a joy when it happens.

And you say that it can

Yet I am still afraid to try – supposing I fail? But you have chosen me, Lord? To open the door for you to reach someone?

You trust me?

Then I can become strong enough for the work. I will do it for You - and for him, for her, for them.

In the *silence* let me think on Christ's trust . . .

Reflections

Matthew 3.7-11

When John saw many Pharisees and Sadducees coming to him to be baptized, he said to them, 'You snakes - who told you that you could escape from the punishment God is about to send? Do those things that will show that you have turned from your sins. And don't think you can escape punishment by saying that Abraham is your ancestor. I tell you that God can take these stones and make descendants for Abraham! The axe is ready to cut down the trees at the roots; every tree that does not bear good fruit will be cut down and thrown in the fire. I baptize you with water to show that you have repented, but the one who will come after me will baptize you with the Holy Spirit and fire. He is much greater than I am; and I am not good enough even to carry his sandals.'

Think on Christ

DAY 2

HIS COMING IS FOR BAPTISM

That was a long time ago, Lord; that was John the Baptist speaking to the Pharisees and Saducees.

Surely you are not saying the same thing to me today?

Will you baptise me with the Holy Spirit? Can I share in your power
to love even the unlovable,
to forgive even the worst that anyone has done to me,
to be patient even with the most difficult people,
to be able to bring order out of chaos?

Lord, it sounds too good to be true.

But I want to be like that.

Make me ready to accept your spirit.

Will you baptise me with the fire
that burns away the falseness in me,
that gives me light and guidance for the future,
that warms my heart towards my neighbour?

I cannot have your spirit and not your fire, can I?

Then let me be willing to bear the fire, too.

Lord, baptise me - please

In the *silence* let me think on Christ's baptism . . .

Matthew 4.1-11

Then the Spirit led Jesus into the desert to be tempted by the Devil. After spending forty days and nights without food, Jesus was hungry. Then the Devil came to him and said, 'If you are God's Son, order these stones to turn into bread.'

But Jesus answered, 'The scripture says, "Man cannot live on bread alone, but needs every word that God speaks."'

Then the Devil took Jesus to Jerusalem, the Holy City, set him on the highest point of the temple, and said to him, 'If you are God's Son, throw yourself down, for the scripture says,

"God will give orders to his angels about you;
they will hold you up with their hands,
so that not even your feet will be hurt on the stones."'

Jesus answered, 'But the scripture also says, "Do not put the Lord your God to the test."'

Then the Devil took Jesus to a very high mountain and showed him all the kingdoms of the world in all their greatness. 'All this I will give you,' the Devil said, 'if you kneel down and worship me.'

Then Jesus answered, 'Go away, Satan! The scripture says, "Worship the Lord your God and serve only him!"'

Then the Devil left Jesus; and angels came and helped him.

Think on Christ

DAY 3

HIS MOTIVES TESTED

No sooner had your Father said 'This is my own dear Son, with whom I am pleased', than you were put to the test. You were prepared to give everything for humankind, and then came your struggle.

You won your battle; you refused to make any compromise; you were your Father's servant, and the only methods you could use to fulfil His purpose would have to be His.

Lord Jesus Christ,
when you give me any task, and show me how to achieve it,
save me from trying to take short cuts;
when my motives are tested, hold me firm to the highest;
when I hear the world telling me to use my common-sense,
help me to hear your powerful word;
give me the confidence to know that if I follow your
commands, it is all that you ask of me; success or failure
are no longer in my hands;
be with me in my testing times, and bring me through them
better fitted to be a servant in the Kingdom of your Father.

In the *silence* let me think on Christ's testing . . .

Reflections

Matthew 4.18-22

As Jesus walked along the shore of Lake Galilee, he saw two brothers who were fishermen, Simon (called Peter) and his brother Andrew, catching fish in the lake with a net. Jesus said to them, 'Come with me, and I will teach you to catch men.' At once they left their nets and went with him.

He went on and saw two other brothers, James and John, the sons of Zebedee. They were in their boat with their father Zebedee, getting their nets ready. Jesus called them, and at once they left the boat and their father, and went with him.

Think on Christ

DAY 4

FISHERS OF MEN

You promised to make those fishermen fishers of men. They accepted your offer and your promise came true.

What are you offering me? Do you want to make me something other than I am? It would be arrogant to think that you were satisfied with me. Even I am not pleased with what I am, but the will and the effort to be different is often missing. I have had dreams of the new person I might be, but they have faded away.

Do I have to try harder? Do I set myself new objectives and struggle to reach them? I have done that before and it does not seem to work.

> Now I see, I've got it the wrong way round. You didn't say 'Make yourselves fishers of men' but 'I will make you fishers of men'.

Lord, I will start again from that point; now I can listen. You surely have something, someone for me to be; I can rely upon you to achieve your purpose in me. All you need, right now, is my surrender to your purpose.

I give myself over to you, please make me. You are making me.

In the *silence* let me think on Christ's will . . .

Matthew 5.40-41

And if someone takes you to court to sue you for your shirt, let him have your coat as well. And if one of the occupation troops forces you to carry his pack one kilometre, carry it two kilometres.

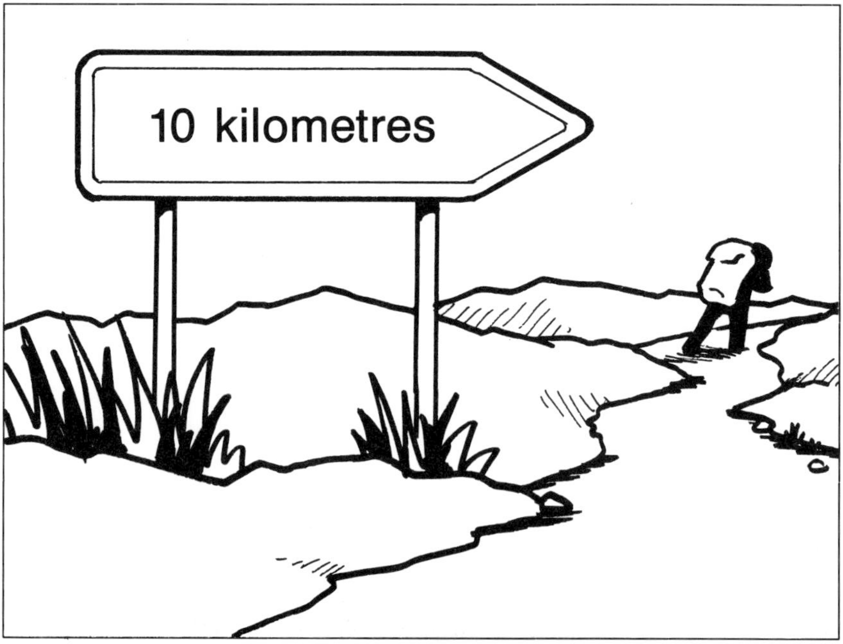

Think on Christ

DAY 5

THE SECOND KILOMETRE

Lord Jesus, you don't make it very easy to be a Christian, do you? It's hard enough to do what I must do, but to volunteer to go beyond that limit is asking more than is reasonable.

But who is asking me to go the second kilometre?
my husband,
my wife,
my friend,
my neighbour,
my boss?

'Not them only' you say, 'A second kilometre for me'

I can't refuse that. You go the second kilometre, and more, for me. You never set limits on your service to me even when I am ungrateful.

A second kilometre for You. That makes all the difference.

Whoever wants me to go a kilometre, I will go a kilometre and willingly go a second for him or her but most of all, for you.

In the *silence* let me think on Christ's way . . .

Matthew 6.1-4

'Make certain you do not perform your religious duties in public so that people will see what you do. If you do these things publicly, you will not have any reward from your Father in heaven.

So when you give something to a needy person, do not make a big show of it, as the hypocrites do in the houses of worship and on the streets. They do it so that people will praise them. I assure you, they have already been paid in full. But when you help a needy person, do it in such a way that even your closest friend will not know about it. Then it will be a private matter, and your Father, who sees what you do in private, will reward you.'

Think on Christ

DAY 6

GRATITUDE

Lord, I don't want any publicity for the good I did - or do I? No illuminated address or vote of thanks or even a presentation, nothing elaborate. That's not what I'm after. But it would be nice to have a 'Thankyou', a letter or a phone call.

When I'm unsure that what I do for others is really appreciated, it makes it difficult to help them again.

Is it wrong to expect some acknowledgement?

Perhaps they are not thankful to me;
perhaps they did not want to be 'done good' to;
now that I think about it, I wonder if it was really for me that I did it, so that I could feel good, or just that little bit superior;
maybe it's just as well no-one has said anything about it, it might not bear looking at too closely.

Another thing, Lord; all this reminds me that I have not always been as thankful to you as I might have been, taking many of your gifts for granted as if I had a right to expect them.

Forgive me for seeming to be ungrateful, and help me to realise how much I owe you for all your loving.

In the *silence* let me think on Christ's giving . . .

Reflections

Matthew 6.5-8

'When you pray, do not be like the hypocrites! They love to stand up and pray in the houses of worship and on the street corners, so that everyone will see them. I assure you, they have already been paid in full. But when you pray, go to your room, close the door, and pray to your Father, who is unseen. And your Father, who sees what you do in private, will reward you.

When you pray, do not use a lot of meaningless words, as the pagans do, who think that their Gods will hear them because their prayers are long. Do not be like them. Your Father already knows what you need before you ask him.'

Think on Christ

DAY 7

HOW NOT TO PRAY

Lord, I am the last one to want to parade my religion. I am not likely to pray on the street corner. It is not often that I stand up in church to pray either, not unless you include some of the hymns. I'm much more likely to do as you said I should:

'Go to your room, close the door
and pray to your Father, who is unseen'

It looks as if I have got it right!

But saying that means that I have fallen into the trap of self-righteousness. So, I must start again.

Teach me, Lord, how to pray.
Keep me from talking and not listening.
Stop me from seeking gifts from you, and not giving myself to you,
Yet may I remember that you are always more willing to give than I am to receive.
When I repent may I sincerely want to give up sinning.
When you give me forgiveness let me live as if I really had been set free.
When I ask for gifts for others don't let me think that there is nothing left for me to do.

It isn't easy, Lord, go on teaching me how to pray.

In the *silence* let me think on Christ's teaching . . .

Matthew 7.7-11

'Ask, and you will receive; seek, and you will find; knock, and the door will be opened to you. For everyone who asks will receive, and anyone who seeks will find, and the door will be opened to him who knocks. Would any of you who are fathers give your son a stone when he asks for bread? Or would you give him a snake when he asks for a fish? Bad as you are, you know how to give good things to your children. How much more, then, will you Father in heaven give good things to those who ask him!'

Think on Christ

DAY 8

ASK, SEEK, KNOCK

I'd like to believe that things work out as simply as that.
Asking, and receiving;
seeking, and finding;
knocking, and the door opening.

Often I have,
asked and have not received;
sought and have not found;
been persistent in knocking, and the door has remained tight shut.

But, come to think of it, I am grateful that it has been that way.
If you had given me all I asked for, I wouldn't have been able to handle it;
if you had let me find everything I sought for, I would often have been overwhelmed;
if you had opened every door I knocked on, I would have become trapped in a maze of my own making.

You are far wiser and loving to me than I am to myself.

I will go on,
asking and be grateful for whatever you give;
seeking and will treasure whatever you reveal;
knocking and be ready to go through any door you open to me.

In the *silence* let me think on Christ's wisdom . . .

Reflections

Matthew 8.5-13

When Jesus entered Capernaum, a Roman officer met him and begged for help: 'Sir, my servant is sick in bed at home, unable to move and suffering terribly.'

'I will go and make him well,' Jesus said.

'Oh no, sir,' answered the officer. 'I do not deserve to have you come into my house. Just give the order, and my servant will get well. I, too, am a man under the authority of superior officers, and I have soldiers under me. I order this one, "Go!" and he goes; and I order that one, "Come!" and he comes; and I order my slave, "Do this!" and he does it.'

When Jesus heard this, he was surprised and said to the people following him, 'I tell you, I have never found anyone in Israel with faith like this. I assure you that many will come from the east and the west and sit down with Abraham, Isaac, and Jacob at the feast in the Kingdom of heaven. But those who should be in the Kingdom will be thrown out into the darkness, where they will cry and grind their teeth.' Then Jesus said to the officer, 'Go home, and what you believe will be done for you.'

And the officer's servant was healed that very moment.

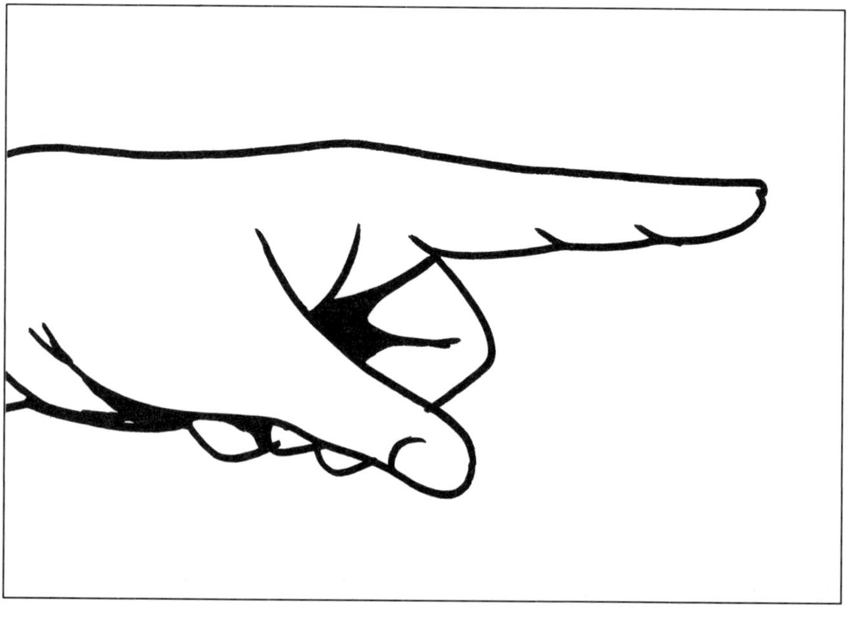

Think on Christ

DAY 9

RECOGNITION OF AUTHORITY

It wasn't easy for this Roman soldier to come asking for your help, was it? He must have had a deep affection for his servant. He did not try to curry favour with you. He didn't make any promises. Stories about your power had gripped him; what you had done for others you could do for this 'slave'.

He recognised you as a man with authority.

I don't always see you like that. Perhaps that is why I am reluctant to ask you what you require from me. If I did ask, I would be afraid that I might get an unacceptable answer.

You might ask,
something beyond my reach,
something I've been avoiding,
something that others would not accept,
something that would mean I have to change the pattern of my life.

Lord, I know you called your disciples friends, but they still regarded themselves as servants too. I am your servant.

Whatever you ask of me;
whether it is public or private,
whether it is major or minor,
whether I like it or not.

Be my authority, then I know I am on the right lines.

In the *silence* let me think on Christ's authority . . .

Matthew 8.28-34

When Jesus came to the territory of Gadara on the other side of the lake, he was met by two men who came out of the burial caves there. These men had demons in them and were so fierce that no one dared travel on that road. At once they screamed, 'What do you want with us, you Son of God? Have you come to punish us before the right time?'

Not far away there was a large herd of pigs feeding. So the demons begged Jesus, 'If you are going to drive us out, send us into that herd of pigs.'

'Go,' Jesus told them; so they left and went off into the pigs. The whole herd rushed down the side of the cliff into the lake and was drowned.

The men who had been taking care of the pigs ran away and went into the town, where they told the whole story and what had happened to the men with the demons. So everyone from the town went out to meet Jesus; and when they saw him, they begged him to leave their territory.

PLEASE GO AWAY

Lord Jesus, I can't imagine that I would ever reject you. But I must admit that there are times when I wish that I could forget or ignore you, times when I feel that life would be easier without your involvement.

I planned a holiday, no-one would blame me for that; but you came and showed me a hungry child.

I was asked to serve your church. I said I didn't have time; but as I was watching the television serial you faced me.

At the moment when my neighbour had strained my patience to breaking point, I heard you say 'Love your neighbour'. The preacher said that one of the marks of the true Christian is the spirit of sacrifice.

I rebelled. Give reasonably – yes; sacrificially – no.

But then I saw you on the Cross

Please go away. I can't bear it. But, Lord I couldn't bear it if you did leave me. Stay with me and make me whole.

In the *silence* let me think on Christ's healing . . .

Matthew 9.1-8

Jesus got into the boat and went back across the lake to his own town, where some people brought to him a paralysed man, lying on a bed. When Jesus saw how much faith they had, he said to the paralysed man, 'Courage, my son! Your sins are forgiven.'

Then some teachers of the Law said to themselves, 'This man is speaking blasphemy!'

Jesus perceived what they were thinking, so he said, 'Why are you thinking such evil things? Is it easier to say, "Your sins are forgiven," or to say, "Get up and walk?" I will prove to you, then, that the Son of Man has authority on earth to forgive sins.' So he said to the paralysed man, 'Get up, pick up your bed, and go home!'

The man got up and went home. When the people saw it, they were afraid, and praised God for giving such authority to men.

BROUGHT

Some people brought a paralysed man to you, Lord. You forgave his sins and you healed him. His friends were looking for one gift and you gave two. That is so like you Lord. Your generosity exceeds all that we can anticipate.

How many of my friends - friends who needed help to come to you - have I brought?

Some are reluctant, even resistant.
Do I just leave them?
Do I go on and on trying or do I give up?

Some don't believe that you can do anything for them.
Are there ways in which I can convince them?

Some are afraid that you might bring about a change they do not want.
How can I help them overcome their fear?

Some want to go their own way - they do not want my 'interference'.
Is it right for me to allow them to go on without coming face to face with you?

It is wonderful to have friends, and family, but when I cannot get them to meet you, I feel a failure.

Show me what to do and what not to do. Show me how they may be brought to you.

In the *silence* let me think on Christ's receiving . . .

Reflections

Matthew 9.10-13

While Jesus was having a meal in Matthew's house, many tax collectors and other outcasts came and joined Jesus and his disciples at the table. Some Pharisees saw this and asked his disciples, 'Why does your teacher eat with such people?'

Jesus heard them and answered, 'People who are well do not need a doctor, but only those who are sick. Go and find out what is meant by the scripture that says: "It is kindness that I want, not animal sacrifices." I have not come to call respectable people, but outcasts.'

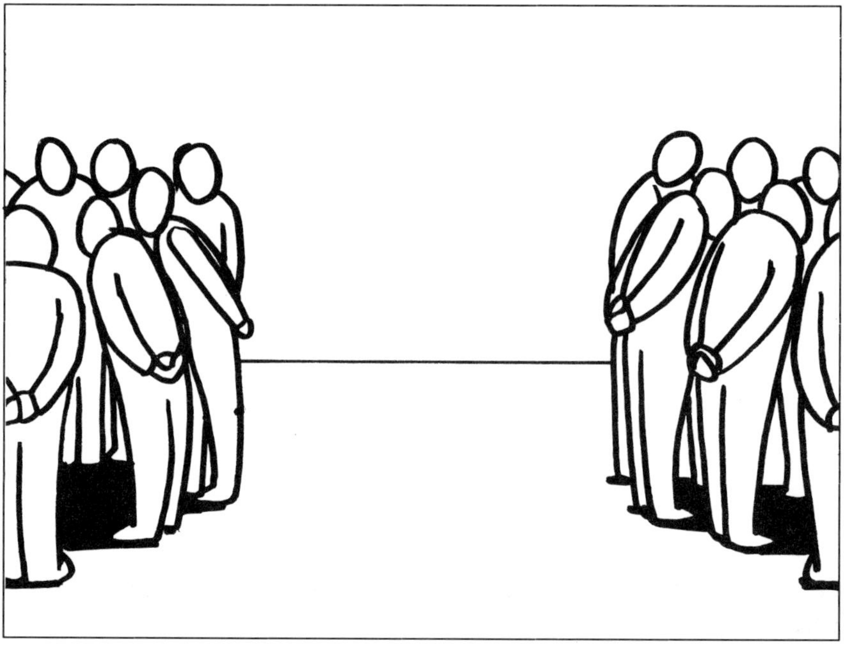

Think on Christ

DAY 12

THEM AND US

Lord Jesus, is that really where you had to be? With tax-gatherers and unrepentant sinners? Is that where you are now? If you are, it is not surprising that we do not meet you very often.

It is so much easier to be with,
  people of good intentions;
  those who think as we do;
  those who have the same standards as we have;
  those who are loyal to your Church.

We seldom come across "the others" and if we do it is only by accident and we get away as soon as we can.

It is difficult neither to sound, nor to be, patronising. Help us to learn how to serve others and not to make them feel that we think they are less worthy than we are. We need to learn why they live the way they do, or what has forced them into their attitudes.

Teach us that in your sight there are not two categories - some who belong to you and some who do not.

Lord, not 'I' and 'they', but 'we'.

In the *silence* let me think on Christ's all embracing love . . .

Matthew 11.1-6

When Jesus finished giving these instructions to his twelve disciples, he left that place and went off to teach and preach in the towns near there.

When John the Baptist heard in prison about the things that Christ was doing, he sent some of his disciples to him. 'Tell us,' they asked Jesus, 'are you the one John said was going to come, or should we expect someone else?'

Jesus answered, 'Go back and tell John what you are hearing and seeing: the blind can see, the lame can walk, those who suffer from dreaded skin-diseases are made clean, the deaf hear, the dead are brought back to life, and the Good News is preached to the poor. How happy are those who have no doubts about me!'

WHAT IS YOUR EVIDENCE?

Wherever you went, Lord Jesus, things happened. Blind people were given back their sight. Lame people were able to walk again. Lepers were cured. The deaf could hear again. The dead were given new life.

The Good News was preached to the poor.

It must have been a wonderful time to wake up every day knowing that you were there. The results of your power at work were there for all to see, so that anyone could believe – but they didn't.

They saw miracles but did not believe. I do not always believe, but I don't see you perform miracles to help me to believe.

You have not given up;
You are alive in our world;
You are willing to be active in my world, however small it may be.

That is where the miracles could take place – that is where you want them to happen.

You ask from me one single thing – faith.

Is it so difficult a thing you ask; so difficult for me to give?

Lord, I do believe - in you and in your power to perform miracles.

In the *silence* let me think on Christ's miraculous powers . . .

Matthew 11.19

'When the Son of Man came, he ate and drank, and everyone said, "Look at this man! He is a glutton and a drinker, a friend of tax collectors and other outcasts!" God's wisdom, however, is shown to be true by it's results.'

Think on Christ
DAY 14

HE CAME EATING AND DRINKING

Eating and drinking, just like everyone else!

> I know you weren't. You were unique. There never had been, nor has been since, anyone like you.

But you were human. You had feelings and experiences like ours, and showed us how to live with them, to accept them, to conquer them, and to hope in spite of them.

You were hungry and thirsty;
you were weary;
you rejoiced;
you were angry and disappointed;
you were lonely;
you suffered and died.

Today you know the pattern of my life and share it with me. You know the heights and depths. Nothing is foreign to you.

> My life is a shared life.

You know what it is like,
when people misinterpret my best intentions, my sincerest motives,
when I have tried to present your truth clearly and people remain indifferent,
when I am suffering pain; it's all mine and no-one can take even a fragment from me,
when I am worn out with work and someone asks for more from me,
when I face death and I must leave this life with so much I wanted to do unaccomplished,
when I find joy and peace in living, and all things seem worthwhile.

You know the human frame, the mind and spirit. You are ready to participate in mine.

> I need never live alone.

In the *silence* let me think on Christ's humanity . . .

Reflections

Matthew 11.28-30

'Come to me, all of you who are tired from carrying heavy loads, and I will give you rest. Take my yoke and put it on you, and learn from me, because I am gentle and humble in spirit; and you will find rest. For the yoke I will give you is easy, and the load I will put on you is light.'

Think on Christ

DAY 15

I NEED A REST

All of us! What a mighty promise, Lord. Not one of us excluded from this priceless gift of rest. How I need to be sure that I can depend on this fact;
when I am restless,
when I feel at breaking point,
when I am tired out,
when I have no more resources,
when everything is too much.

I must be sure that someone is prepared and able to bear my burden with me, and you promise always to be that someone.

Nothing is too insignificant, nothing too great.

You offer me your yoke. You knew how to carry your burdens; your yoke of faith in the Father was so well-fitting, so strong, that you could bear anything –
Rejection
Hypocrisy
Ignorance
Contempt
Strife
Death

All of this and more you carried, and still you were not bowed down.

You were strong enough for all burdens.

That's the kind of yoke I need – your yoke of faith – I will take it today. Thank you Lord.

In the *silence* let me think on Christ's yoke of faith . . .

Matthew 13.33

Jesus told them still another parable: 'The Kingdom of heaven is like this. A woman takes some yeast and mixes it with forty litres of flour until the whole batch of dough rises.'

Think on Christ

DAY 16

TAKE SOME YEAST

Lord Jesus, your Father's kingdom is around me and within me, yet it remains a mystery.

I don't know how it functions, I can't always see it at work.

The yeast of
love turns strife into peace;
obedience turns despair into confidence;
trust turns agitation into patience;
hope turns fear into courage
comfort turns sorrow into joy.

Your transforming spirit always works. If only I were open to the yeast of the kingdom, there would be within me changes for good; but I resist change.

If I yield to your transforming spirit I must learn your new ways.

Your yeast is always good; it always brings a new quality of life – your life.

Make me ready to welcome the yeast of the Gospel into the whole of my being so that every day I grow towards the fullness you have chosen for me.

In the *silence* let me think on Christ's uplifting power . . .

Matthew 13.45-46

'Also, the Kingdom of heaven is like this. A man is looking for fine pearls, and when he finds one that is unusually fine, he goes and sells everything he has, and buys that pearl.'

Think on Christ

DAY 17

NOTHING MORE VALUABLE

There are many things that matter to me – family, friends, church, books, work, hobbies, music, art and sport. But more valuable than these is the kingdom. When I know that I am in tune with the kingdom's ways, and that I live by the King's Laws, then I realise that this is a treasure without price.

Life has many riches. Some marvels I have discovered - others still lie hidden from me. Some I have worked to unearth - others have appeared without my effort.

But the greatest of all is the kingdom.

It is very tempting to grasp the good and miss the best. Too often I have been satisfied with medium quality living when I should have longed for the highest. I have been absorbed by the mildly satisfying and have not gone on to the totally fulfilling.

Make me a seeker, Lord,
Give me the ability to discern the finest you provide;
Equip me with the tenacity to overcome the obstacles to discovering your riches;
Stir up in me a healthy dissatisfaction with the mediocre;
Lead me to your kingdom. Today I embark on the search.

In the *silence* let me think on Christ's riches . . .

Matthew 14.13-18

When Jesus heard the news about John, he left there in a boat and went to a lonely place by himself. The people heard about it, so they left their towns and followed him by land. Jesus got out of the boat, and when he saw the large crowd, his heart was filled with pity for them, and he healed those who were ill.

That evening his disciples came to him and said, 'It is already very late, and this is a lonely place. Send the people away and let them go to the villages to buy food for themselves.'

'They don't have to leave,' answered Jesus. 'You yourselves give them something to eat!'

'All we have here are five loaves and two fish,' they replied.

'Then bring them here to me,' Jesus said.

Think on Christ

DAY 18

UNLIMITED SUPPLIES

Lord, it couldn't happen, could it? Just five loaves and two fish, a meal for thousands - it just doesn't make sense. But then I'm forgetting the all-important thing, aren't I? It wasn't just a little bread and fish and a great crowd. You were there too, with all your love and power at work.

You made all the difference; you always do.

If I gave what I had to you, you would show me my hidden resources;
I do not have enough courage, but if I gave it to you,
you would make it sufficient to dare the impossible.
I do not have enough persistence, but if I gave it to
you, you would enlarge it to achieve your will.
I do not have enough tolerance, but if I gave it to you,
you would expand it to bear those things I cannot change.
I do not have enough faith, but if I gave it to you, you
would make it grow until it could move mountains.

What amazing possibilities open out before me, if I give to you what I have - possibilities not only for me but for others.

Take what I have, Lord, and use it.

In the *silence* let me think on Christ's resources . . .

Matthew 16.24-26

Then Jesus said to his disciples, 'If anyone wants to come with me, he must forget self, carry his cross, and follow me. For whoever wants to save his own life will lose it; but whoever loses his life for my sake will find it. Will a person gain anything if he wins the whole world but loses his life? Of course not! There is nothing he can give to regain his life.'

Think on Christ

DAY 19

LOSE TO SAVE

You are telling me that if I want to be a Christian in the fullest possible sense, there are three things I must do.

I must deny myself and say 'Yes' to you. You must be at the centre of my life. Everything I am and do must have you at the heart of it. You take me into the centre of your love – I say 'YES'.

I must take up my cross for I cannot expect to be a Christian without accepting suffering. My life should be lived for others. You took up your cross for me. You chose to suffer for my sake. I take my cross.

I must follow you and wherever you lead I must go. I must keep my eyes fixed on you. I must always take you as my guide. You are my Lord and I cannot be disobedient – I will follow you.

Thank you, Lord, for telling me again how I can know the exhilaration of being a Christian.

In the *silence* let me think on Christ's conditions of service . . .

Matthew 17.1-8

Six days later Jesus took with him Peter and the brothers James and John and led them up a high mountain where they were alone. As they looked on, a change came over Jesus: his face was shining like the sun, and his clothes were dazzling white. Then the three disciples saw Moses and Elijah talking with Jesus. So Peter spoke up and said to Jesus, 'Lord, how good it is that we are here! If you wish, I will make three tents here, one for you, one for Moses, and one for Elijah.'

While he was talking, a shining cloud came over them, and a voice from the cloud said, 'This is my own dear Son, with whom I am pleased - listen to him!'

When the disciples heard the voice, they were so terrified that they threw themselves face downwards on the ground. Jesus came to them and touched them. 'Get up,' he said. 'Don't be afraid!' So they looked up and saw no one there but Jesus.

ON THE MOUNTAIN TOP

It's great to be on a mountain-top with you, Lord; I have had some wonderful hours there with you. I have been able to see you in all your glory. How I have longed to stay up on the heights with you.

But it hasn't worked out that way. I have had to come down into the valley where people demand attention and duties flood in. Sometimes it even seems that I have deceived myself and that I never did come so close to you.

I need the experience of being on the mountain with you.
I want my Christianity to have times of majesty and splendour. I believe you want that for me too – then it will happen. What a marvellous hope.

But I do know that it is not like that all the time.
Sometimes it is plain dull; just doing the same thing all over again.
Sometimes it is painful; I have to carry burdens which threaten to overwhelm me.
Sometimes it lacks all point; it seems as if I'm not getting anywhere.
Sometimes it is frustrating; relentlessly, failure follows failure.

Lord, I accept the mountain-top and the valley, you are in both places – I had forgotten that.

In the *silence* let me think on Christ's vision . . .

Matthew 18.12-14

'What do you think a man does who has a hundred sheep and one of them gets lost? He will leave the other ninety-nine grazing on the hillside and go and look for the lost sheep. When he finds it, I tell you, he feels far happier over this one sheep than over the ninety-nine that did not get lost. In just the same way your Father in heaven does not want any of these little ones to be lost.'

Think on Christ

DAY 21

STRAYED AND FOUND

Lord, there are days when I feel quite sure that I am one of the ninety-nine, safely with the flock.

I have everything I need,
your strength is poured into me;
you guide me in the right ways;
even in the deepest darkness I know you are with me;
I am not afraid.

Everything is so good and so right, that if anyone suggested I might stray I would reject the thought completely. But I know that, in spite of that, I do stray because I choose to ignore your leading. Although I know it brings no final satisfaction, I go my own way.

But still you come looking for me,
you still include me in your flock;
you ignore my careless wandering;
you search me out and draw me back.

Such love is beyond my understanding but I know that it happens.

I am determined not to stray again, but if I do, please come looking for me – for you are my Good Shepherd - and bring me back to your flock.

In the *silence* let me think on Christ's seeking . . .

Matthew 20.29-34

As Jesus and his disciples were leaving Jericho, a large crowd was following. Two blind men who were sitting by the road heard that Jesus was passing by, so they began to shout, 'Son of David! Take pity on us, sir!'

The crowd scolded them and told them to be quiet. But they shouted even more loudly, 'Son of David! Take pity on us, sir!'

Jesus stopped and called them. 'What do you want me to do for you?' he asked them.

'Sir,' they answered, 'we want you to give us our sight!'

Jesus had pity on them and touched their eyes; at once they were able to see, and they followed him.

WHAT DO YOU WANT?

What audacity! What right did those men have to ask you for the gift of sight? Two blind beggars - two among a vast crowd. Why should they expect that you would pay any attention to their needs? They made such an uproar between them that the crowd could not hear what you were saying.

Yet you did listen to them;
you chose to stop and respond to them;
you asked no questions about their sincerity or their worthiness;
you made no bargain with them;
you healed them.

Lord, that sets me free.

I, too, can ask for great gifts,
you will listen to me and respond to me;
you will not demand that I should be faultless or require a payment.

Now I must decide what it is I want, what I need. May I not despise your generosity by asking for an inappropriate gift. Give me the courage to know that I can trust your love.

Whatever I ask that is good for me, I know it is your will to grant.

Help me to ask fearlessly, and to be open to your healing love.

In the *silence* let me think on Christ's healing love . . .

Matthew 21.12-14

Jesus went into the Temple and drove out all those who were buying and selling there. He overturned the tables of the money-changers and the stools of those who sold pigeons, and said to them, 'It is written in the Scriptures that God said, "My Temple will be called a house of prayer." But you are making it a hide-out for thieves!'

The blind and the crippled came to him in the Temple, and he healed them.

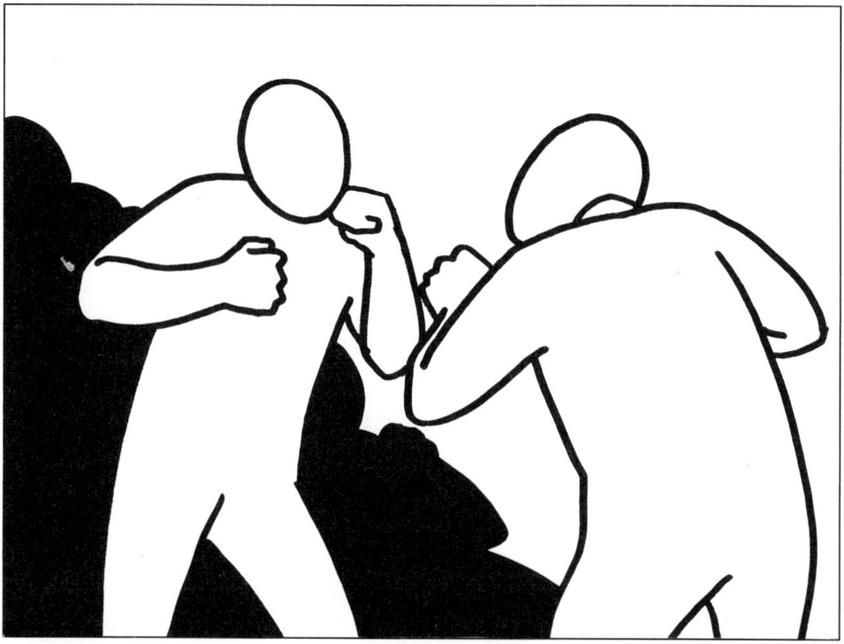

HE IS ANGRY

Do you, like me, have your breaking point, Lord? Are there times when tolerance and patience are no longer possible?

There is one difference between your anger and mine – you are angry for the exploited and with those who abuse the house of prayer. I lose my temper when I am threatened or attacked.

It is surprising how patient I am when it is others who are suffering,
I am tolerant towards those who offend against people far away, or even near at hand;
their pain can be forgotten or absorbed.

Lord, I need to know when to be angry – with whom to be angry – on whose behalf to be angry.

I am afraid of being angry in the wrong place, at the wrong time, for the wrong reason.

I look to you as my guide in this as in all things. Unless I am following where you lead, I am bound to go wrong.

If today,
I am angry - may it be anger like yours;
I ought to be angry - help me to be ready for it;
I have been angry without justification – forgive me, and give me grace to try to right the wrong that I have done.

In the *silence* let me think on Christ's control . . .

Matthew 21.28-32

'Now, what do you think? There was once a man who had two sons. He went to the elder one and said, "Son, go and work in the vineyard today." "I don't want to," he answered, but later he changed his mind and went. Then the father went to the other son and said the same thing. "Yes, sir," he answered, but he did not go. Which one of the two did what his father wanted?'

'The elder one,' they answered.

So Jesus said to them, 'I tell you: the tax collectors and the prostitutes are going into the Kingdom of God ahead of you. For John the Baptist came to you showing you the right path to take, and you would not believe him; but the tax collectors and the prostitutes believed him. Even when you saw this, you did not later change your minds and believe him.'

A REFUSAL AND A PROMISE

No – yes. Yes – no. Yes – yes. It is the third kind of person that you want me to be; so often I am one of the others. When you ask of me what seems beyond me, I refuse. I cannot risk making a fool of myself. I know my limitations and weaknesses. I'm a very ordinary Christian.

But then I know that you will equip me for what you ask; you see me as I could grow to be. So I change my mind.

When you call me to serve you in some simple way, it is obvious that my answer must be 'Yes'. Then, sometimes, I think there are others who could do it better. I must have misheard, you couldn't have meant me. So I change my mind. I am an unreliable servant in either case.

The unaccountable thing is that, in spite of all this, you go on calling me again and again. You must really want me, even need me. I cannot understand that, but who am I to contradict you?

When you call me, let my response be 'Yes'.

In the *silence* let me think on Christ's call . . .

Matthew 23.37-38

'Jerusalem, Jerusalem! You kill the prophets and stone the messengers God has sent you! How many times have I wanted to put my arms round all your people, just as a hen gathers her chicks under her wings, but you would not let me! And so your Temple will be abandoned and empty.'

'YOU WOULD NOT LET ME'

I can almost hear the pain in your voice. You wanted to give yourself to them, but they would not accept you. They could have had love and security unbounded, but they refused it.

Were they afraid?
Were they ashamed?
Did they think they were self-sufficient?
Were they content with a mediocre life?

Even those who claim to know you well still fail to accept you wholly.

Lord, help me to understand how much of life I miss
when I neglect to accept your offer of abundant life.

I could use more **love.**
Hope sometimes drains away.
My **faith** is inadequate to meet my daily needs.
I lack enough **peace** to calm my troubled mind in days of anxiety and turmoil.
Challenged to expand my witness, I do not always have any courage left.

Let me
let you
give me
All You are.

In the *silence* let me think on Christ's offer . . .

Think on Christ

DAY 26

Matthew 25.1-13

'At that time the Kingdom of heaven will be like this. Once there were ten girls who took their oil lamps and went out to meet the bridegroom. Five of them were foolish, and the other five were wise. The foolish ones took their lamps but did not take any extra oil with them, while the wise ones took containers full of oil for their lamps. The bridegroom was late in coming, so the girls began to nod and fall asleep.

It was already midnight when the cry rang out, "Here is the bridegroom! Come and meet him!" The ten girls woke up and trimmed their lamps. Then the foolish ones said to the wise ones, "Let us have some of your oil, because our lamps are going out." "No, indeed," the wise ones answered, "there is not enough for you and for us. Go to the shop and buy some for yourselves." So the foolish girls went off to buy some oil; and while they were gone, the bridegroom arrived. The five girls who were ready went in with him to the wedding feast, and the door was closed.

Later the other girls arrived. "Sir, sir! Let us in!" they cried out. "Certainly not! I don't know you," the bridegroom answered.'

And Jesus concluded, 'Be on your guard, then, because you do not know the day or the hour.'

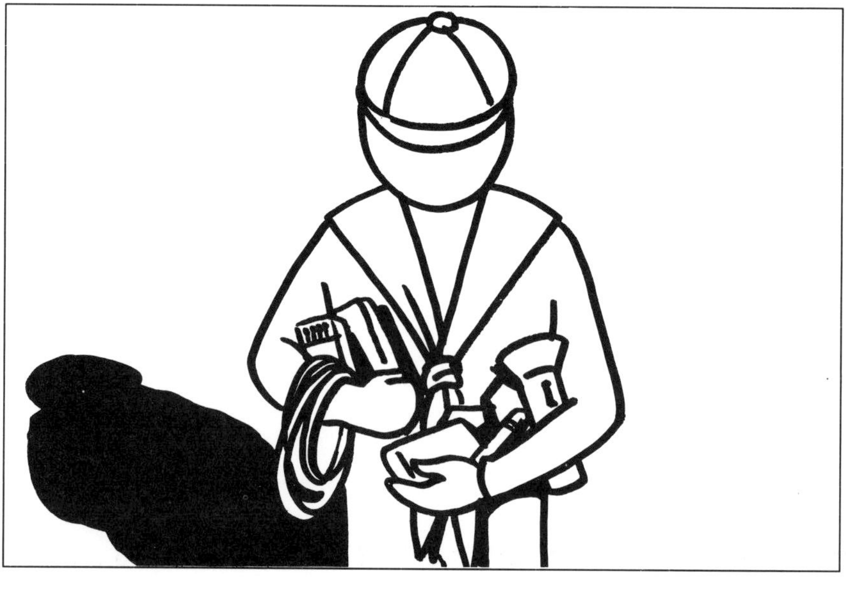

BE PREPARED

I'm often caught out, Lord. I know circumstances might, would, happen one day but I've delayed preparing for them. Opportunities for doing good have to be passed by because I have failed to prepare myself. Death of a loved one finds me unready to trust in your promise of eternal life. I find that people disagree with me, doubt my motives, reject my hopes. I lack the spirit with which you faced the people of Nazareth.

Life goes by and I miss its possibilities.

You told us to have no anxious thought for the morrow, but you didn't mean us to go into the future ill-fitted for its opportunities and its demands, did you?

I have a life to live today. Whatever happens, I need to be prepared if I am to use the day well.

May these coming hours not find me unready to face both known and unknown. You will make that possible, if I am always ready for you.

In the *silence* let me think on Christ's invitation . . .

Think on Christ

DAY 27

Matthew 25.14-30

'At that time the Kingdom of heaven will be like this. Once there was a man who was about to go on a journey; he called his servants and put them in charge of his property. He gave to each one according to his ability: to one he gave five thousand gold coins, to another he gave two thousand, and to another he gave one thousand. Then he left on his journey. The servant who had received five thousand coins went at once and invested his money and earned another five thousand. In the same way the servant who had received two thousand coins earned another two thousand. But the servant who had received one thousand coins went off, dug a hole in the ground, and hid his master's money.

After a long time the master of those servants came back and settled accounts with them. The servant who had received five thousand coins came in and handed over the other five thousand. "You gave me five thousand coins sir," he said. "Look! Here are another five thousand that I have earned." "Well done, you good and faithful servant!" said his master. "You have been faithful in managing small amounts, so I will put you in charge of large amounts. Come on in and share my happiness!"

Then the servant who had been given two thousand coins came in and said, "You gave me two thousand coins, sir. Look! Here are another two thousand that I have earned." "Well done, you good and faithful servant!" said his master. "You have been faithful in managing small amounts, so I will put you in charge of large amounts. Come on in and share my happiness!"

Then the servant who had received one thousand coins came in and said, "Sir, I know you are a hard man; you reap harvests where you did not sow, and you gather crops where you did not scatter seed. I was afraid, so I went off and hid your money in the ground. Look! Here is what belongs to you."

"You bad and lazy servant!" his master said. "You knew, did you, that I reap harvests where I did not sow, and gather crops where I did not scatter seed? Well, then, you should have deposited my money in the bank, and I would have received it all back with interest when I returned. Now, take the money away from him and give it to the one who has ten thousand coins. For to every person who has something, even more will be given, and he will have more than enough; but the person who has nothing, even the little that he has will be taken away from him. As for this useless servant - throw him outside in the darkness; there he will cry and grind his teeth."'

TALENTS MANY, TALENTS FEW

It's no good my claiming that I'm as good as the next man or woman. Many of my neighbours have gifts and abilities that I don't nor ever will have,

some have more imagination than I;
some are more knowledgeable;
next door there's a DIY expert;
down the road there's a great pianist;
around the corner a lady makes her own dresses;
across the way there's an excellent gardener;
I don't seem to be able to be any of these.

I cannot excel at everything. Perhaps I shall never excel at anything. What do you ask of me? Do I hear you aright?

'Use the gifts you do have as fully as you can'. That's a target that I can aim at.

What I can do, I will do; what I cannot do, I will do as well as I can. I will not waste my talents be they many or few.

In the *silence* let me think on Christ's encouragement . . .

Matthew 26.6-13

Jesus was in Bethany at the house of Simon, a man who had suffered from a dreaded skin-disease. While Jesus was eating, a woman came to him with an alabaster jar filled with an expensive perfume, which she poured on his head. The disciples saw this and became angry. 'Why all this waste?' they asked. 'This perfume could have been sold for a large amount and the money give to the poor!'

Jesus knew what they were saying, so he said to them, 'Why are you bothering this woman? It is a fine and beautiful thing she has done for me. You will always have poor people with you, but you will not always have me. What she did was to pour this perfume on my body to get me ready for burial. Now, I assure you that wherever this gospel is preached all over the world, what she has done will be told in memory of her.'

EXTRAVAGANT LOVE

It was a waste. It was extravagant. It was wonderful

Lord, commonsense is so highly praised. It is made to sound as if it were the most commendable of attributes. But there are times when commonsense seems a negligible and even a despicable thing.

It wasn't commonsense for you to dine with society's rejects,
  to touch a leper;
  to let yourself be arrested when you could have avoided it;
  to make a friend of a prostitute;
  to accept the way of the Cross.

But for love, extravagant love, you did all this.

  Is someone waiting for my extravagant love?
  Is there a need that I can never meet by being reasonable?
  Is there a place where I can pour out care in profusion?
  Is there a cause to which I can be generous without
    counting the cost?

Lord, you love me with an extravagant love. Let me not waste it.

In the *silence* let me think on Christ's extravagance . . .

Think on Christ

DAY 29

Matthew 26.26-30

While they were eating, Jesus took a piece of bread, gave a prayer of thanks, broke it, and gave it to his disciples. 'Take and eat it' he said; 'this is my body.'

Then he took a cup, gave thanks to God, and gave it to them. 'Drink it, all of you,' he said; 'this is my blood, which seals God's covenant, my blood poured out for many for the forgiveness of sins. I tell you, I will never again drink this wine until the day I drink the new wine with you in my Father's Kingdom.'

Then they sang a hymn and went out to the Mount of Olives.

BREAD AND WINE

Many books have been written; many sermons have been preached; many dogmas have been constructed; many theologies have been woven from these few words.

I cannot profess to understand everything that has been said about your intentions with this simple act.

But you don't ask for my understanding.

You don't expect me to unravel a problem or to commit myself to a theory. You offer me a covenant. Your appeal is for a response. You draw me into a new relationship.

It is not easy to say 'Lord, I accept your covenant'; I want to prescribe my own terms, to draw my own boundaries. But the covenant is yours; I must accept or reject it; I cannot amend it. I cannot offer an alternative.

You gave yourself without limit; you opened the door to the fact of God's love for **me.** That is what the promise of your covenant means.

A covenant of loving,
of love beyond compare;
of love without end;
of love to the loveless;
of love to everyone;

What better covenant could there be? I accept it as it is.

In the *silence* let me think on Christ's new covenant . . .

Matthew 26.31-35

Then Jesus said to them, 'This very night all of you will run away and leave me, for the scripture says, "God will kill the shepherd, and the sheep of the flock will be scattered." But after I am raised to life, I will go to Galilee ahead of you.'

Peter spoke up and said to Jesus, 'I will never leave you, even though all the rest do!'

Jesus said to Peter, 'I tell you that before the cock crows tonight, you will say three times that you do not know me.'

Peter answered, 'I will never say that, even if I have to die with you!'

And all the other disciples said the same thing.

YOU CAN COUNT ON ME

Peter meant what he said, didn't he? There was no bluffing in his attitude? But we know he was wrong. His promise was bigger than his performance. When the time came, he failed you. Which was the real Peter, Lord; Peter the courageous, or Peter the coward?

That's the way it is with me. There's more than one me.

I mean to be consistent, totally loyal to you under all circumstances. But when the times of testing come, I do not always stand firm. Which is the real me? Or am I both?

I know which one I want to be, and the one you want me to be. I rejoice because I know you strive with me to create the best in me. Day by day you continue in love, patience and forgiveness, making me and re-making me.

You look through
  my weakness and see the strength;
  my foolishness and see wisdom;
  my betrayals and see faithfulness.

Help me to recognise the 'me' that is and the 'me' that by your Spirit could yet be. Please, move me towards the 'me' that you are creating.

In the *silence* let me think on Christ's insight . . .

Matthew 26.36-39

Then Jesus went with his disciples to a place called Gethsemane, and he said to them, 'Sit here while I go over there and pray.' He took with him Peter and the two sons of Zebedee. Grief and anguish came over him, and he said to them, 'The sorrow in my heart is so great that it almost crushes me. Stay here and keep watch with me.'

He went a little farther on, threw himself face downwards on the ground, and prayed, 'My Father, if it is possible, take this cup of suffering from me! Yet not what I want, but what you want.'

YOUR WILL, NOT MINE

Lord, it is good to know that even you had to struggle to achieve obedience.

It brings you so close to me.

Sometimes there is nothing I would rather do than obey our Father in every detail of life. At others I fall far short. Sometimes it seems His will restricts my freedom to explore and experience His wonderful world.

There are things that attract me that He forbids. Why? There are things that I don't want to do. He asks me to make sacrifices, to give time, thought, energy to others.

You surrendered. You obeyed. You chose His will because you loved Him, because you knew that He loved you.

Lord, if I loved, if I was so confident that He loved me, even if I struggled, my response would always be,

'Your will be done'.

In the *silence* let me think on Christ's obedience . . .

PRAYERS FOR THE CHURCH COMMUNITY
PRAYERS
FOR
THE CHURCH
COMMUNITY
COMPILED BY
ROY CHAPMAN & DONALD HILTON